Songs from Vagabondia

Bliss Carman
and Richard Hovey

To H.F.W., for debts of love unpaid,
Her boys inscribe this book that they have made.

CONTENTS.

VAGABONDIA.

Off with the fetters
That chafe and restrain!
Off with the chain!
Here Art and Letters,
Music and wine,
And Myrtle and Wanda,
The winsome witches,
Blithely combine.
Here are true riches,
Here is Golconda,
Here are the Indies,
Here we are free—
Free as the wind is,
Free, as the sea.
Free!

Houp-la!

What have we
To do with the way
Of the Pharisee?
We go or we stay
At our own sweet will;
We think as we say,
And we say or keep still
At our own sweet will,
At our own sweet will.

Here we are free
To be good or bad,
Sane or mad,
Merry or grim
As the mood may be, —
Free as the whim
Of a spook on a spree, —
Free to be oddities,
Not mere commodities,
Stupid and salable,
Wholly available,

1

Ranged upon shelves;
Each with his puny form
In the same uniform,
Cramped and disabled;
We are not labelled,
We are ourselves.

Here is the real,
Here the ideal;
Laughable hardship
Met and forgot,
Glory of bardship—
World's bloom and world's blot;
The shock and the jostle,
The mock and the push,
But hearts like the throstle
A-joy in the bush;
Wits that would merrily
Laugh away wrong,
Throats that would verily
Melt Hell in Song.

What though the dimes be
Elusive as rhymes be,
And Bessie, with finger
Uplifted, is warning
That breakfast next morning
(A subject she's scorning)
Is mighty uncertain!

What care we? Linger
A moment to kiss—
No time's amiss
To a vagabond's ardor—
Thee finish the larder
And pull down the curtain.

Unless ere the kiss come,
Black Richard or Bliss come,
Or Tom with a flagon,
Or Karl with a jag on—
Then up and after
The joy of the night

With the hounds of laughter
To follow the flight
Of the fox-foot hours
That double and run
Through brakes and bowers
Of folly and fun.

With the comrade heart
For a moment's play,
And the comrade heart
For a heavier day,
And the comrade heart
Forever and aye.

For the joy of wine
Is not for long;
And the joy of song
Is a dream of shine;
But the comrade heart
Shall outlast art
And a woman's love
The fame thereof.

But wine for a sign
Of the love we bring!
And song for an oath
That Love is king!
And both, and both
For his worshipping!

Then up and away
Till the break of day,
With a heart that's merry,
And a Tom-and-Jerry,
And a derry-down-derry—
What's that you say.
You highly respectable
Buyers and sellers?
We should be decenter?
Not as we please inter
Custom, frugality,
Use and morality
In the delectable

Depths of wine-cellars?

Midnights of revel,
And noondays of song!
Is it so wrong?
Go to the Devil!

I tell you that we,
While you are smirking
And lying and shirking
life's duty of duties,
Honest sincerity,
We are in verity
Free!
Free to rejoice
In blisses and beauties!
Free as the voice
Of the wind as it passes!
Free as the bird
In the weft of the grasses!
Free as the word
Of the sun to the sea —
Free!

A WAIF.

Do you know what it is to be vagrant born?
A waif is only a waif. And so,
For another idle hour I sit,
In large content while the fire burns low.

I gossip here to my crony heart
Of the day just over, and count it one
Of the royal elemental days,
Though its dreams were few and its deeds were none.

Outside, the winter; inside, the warmth
And a sweet oblivion of turmoil. Why?
All for a gentle girlish hand
With its warm and lingering good-bye.

THE JOYS OF THE ROAD.

Now the joys of the road are chiefly these:
A crimson touch on the hard-wood trees;

A vagrant's morning wide and blue,
In early fall when the wind walks, too;

A shadowy highway cool and brown,
Alluring up and enticing down

From rippled water to dappled swamp,
From purple glory to scarlet pomp;

The outward eye, the quiet will,
And the striding heart from hill to hill;

The tempter apple over the fence;
The cobweb bloom on the yellow quince;

The palish asters along the wood, —
A lyric touch of the solitude;

An open hand, an easy shoe.
And a hope to make the day go through, —

Another to sleep with, and a third
To wake me up at the voice of a bird;

The resonant far-listening morn,
And the hoarse whisper of the corn;

The crickets mourning their comrades lost,
In the night's retreat from the gathering frost;

(Or is it their slogan, plaintive and shrill,
As they beat on their corselets, valiant still?)

A hunger fit for the kings of the sea,
And a loaf of bread for Dickon and me;

Songs from Vagabondia

A thirst like that of the Thirsty Sword,
And a jug of cider on the board;

An idle noon, a bubbling spring,
The sea in the pine-tops murmuring;

A scrap of gossip at the ferry;
A comrade neither glum nor merry,

Asking nothing, revealing naught,
But minting his words from a fund of thought,

A keeper of silence eloquent,
Needy, yet royally well content,

Of the mettled breed, yet abhorring strife,
And full of the mellow juice of life;

A taster of wine, with an eye for a maid,
Never too bold, and never afraid,

Never heart-whole, never heart-sick,
(These are the things I worship in Dick)

No fidget and no reformer, just
A calm observer of ought and must,

A lover of books, but a reader of man,
No cynic and no charlatan,

Who never defers and never demands,
But, smiling, takes the world in his hands, —

Seeing it good as when God first saw
And gave it the weight of his will for law.

And O the joy that is never won,
But follows and follows the journeying sun,

By marsh and tide, by meadow and stream,
A will-o'-the-wind, a light-o'-dream,

Delusion afar, delight anear,

From morrow to morrow, from year to year,

A jack-o'-lantern, a fairy fire,
A dare, a bliss, and a desire!

The racy smell of the forest loam,
When the stealthy, sad-heart leaves go home;

(O leaves, O leaves, I am one with you,
Of the mould and the sun and the wind and the dew!)

The broad gold wake of the afternoon;
The silent fleck of the cold new moon;

The sound of the hollow sea's release
From stormy tumult to starry peace;

With only another league to wend;
And two brown arms at the journey's end!

These are the joys of the open road—
For him who travels without a load.

EVENING ON THE POTOMAC.

The fervid breath of our flushed Southern May
Is sweet upon the city's throat and lips,
As a lover's whose tired arm slips
Listlessly over the shoulder of a queen.

Far away
The river melts in the unseen.
Oh, beautiful Girl-City, how she dips
Her feet in the stream
With a touch that is half a kiss and half a dream!
Her face is very fair,
With flowers for smiles and sunlight in her hair.

My westland flower-town, how serene she is!
Here on this hill from which I look at her,
All is still as if a worshipper
Left at some shrine his offering.

Soft winds kiss
My cheek with a slow lingering.
A luring whisper where the laurels stir
Wiles my heart back to woodland-ward again.

But lo,
Across the sky the sunset couriers run,
And I remain
To watch the imperial pageant of the Sun
Mock me, an impotent Cortez here below,
With splendors of its vaster Mexico.

O Eldorado of the templed clouds!
O golden city of the western sky!
Not like the Spaniard would I storm thy gates;
Not like the babe stretch chubby hands and cry

To have thee for a toy; but far from crowds,
Like my Faun brother in the ferny glen,
Peer from the wood's edge while thy glory waits,
And in the darkening thickets plunge again.

SPRING SONG.

Make me over, mother April,
When the sap begins to stir!
When thy flowery hand delivers
All the mountain-prisoned rivers,
And thy great heart beats and quivers,
To revive the days that were,
Make me over, mother April,
When the sap begins to stir!

Take my dust and all my dreaming,
Count my heart-beats one by one,
Send them where the winters perish;
Then some golden noon recherish
And restore them in the sun,
Flower and scent and dust and dreaming,
With their heart-beats every one!

Set me in the urge and tide-drift
Of the streaming hosts a-wing!
Breast of scarlet, throat of yellow,
Raucous challenge, wooings mellow —
Every migrant is my fellow,
Making northward with the spring.
Loose me in the urge and tide-drift
Of the streaming hosts a-wing!

Shrilling pipe or fluting whistle,
In the valleys come again;
Fife of frog and call of tree-toad,
All my brothers, five or three-toed,
With their revel no more vetoed,
Making music in the rain;
Shrilling pipe or fluting whistle,
In the valleys come again.

Make me of thy seed to-morrow,
When the sap begins to stir!
Tawny light-foot, sleepy bruin,
Bright-eyes in the orchard ruin,

Gnarl the good life goes askew in,
Whiskey-jack, or tanager, —
Make me anything to-morrow,
When the sap begins to stir!

Make me even (How do I know?)
Like my friend the gargoyle there;
It may be the heart within him
Swells that doltish hands should pin him
Fixed forever in mid-air.
Make me even sport for swallows,
Like the soaring gargoyle there!

Give me the old clue to follow,
Through the labyrinth of night!
Clod of clay with heart of fire,
Things that burrow and aspire,
With the vanishing desire,
For the perishing delight, —
Only the old clue to follow,
Through the labyrinth of night!

Make me over, mother April,
When the sap begins to stir!
Fashion me from swamp or meadow,
Garden plot or ferny shadow,
Hyacinth or humble burr!
Make me over, mother April,
When the sap begins to stir!

Let me hear the far, low summons,
When the silver winds return;
Rills that run and streams that stammer,
Goldenwing with his loud hammer,
Icy brooks that brawl and clamor,
Where the Indian willows burn;
Let me hearken to the calling,
When the silver winds return,

Till recurring and recurring,
Long since wandered and come back,
Like a whim of Grieg's or Gounod's,
This same self, bird, bud, or Bluenose,

Some day I may capture (Who knows?)
Just the one last joy I lack,
Waking to the far new summons,
When the old spring winds come back.

For I have no choice of being,
When the sap begins to climb, —
Strong insistence, sweet intrusion,
Vasts and verges of illusion, —
So I win, to time's confusion,
The one perfect pearl of time,
Joy and joy and joy forever,
Till the sap forgets to climb!

Make me over in the morning
From the rag-bag of the world!
Scraps of dream and duds of daring,
Home-brought stuff from far sea-faring,
Faded colors once so flaring,
Shreds of banners long since furled!
Hues of ash and glints of glory,
In the rag-bag of the world!

Let me taste the old immortal
Indolence of life once more;
Not recalling nor foreseeing,
Let the great slow joys of being
Well my heart through as of yore!
Let me taste the old immortal
Indolence of life once more!

Give me the old drink for rapture,
The delirium to drain,
All my fellows drank in plenty
At the Three Score Inns and Twenty
From the mountains to the main!
Give me the old drink for rapture,
The delirium to drain!

Only make me over, April,
When the sap begins to stir!
Make me man or make me woman,
Make me oaf or ape or human,

Cup of flower or cone of fir;
Make me anything but neuter
When the sap begins to stir!

THE FAUN. A FRAGMENT.

I will go out to grass with that old King,
For I am weary of clothes and cooks.
I long to lie along the banks of brooks,
And watch the boughs above me sway and swing.
Come, I will pluck off custom's livery,
Nor longer be a lackey to old Time.
Time shall serve me, and at my feet shall fling
The spoil of listless minutes. I shall climb
The wild trees for my food, and run
Through dale and upland as a fox runs free,
Laugh for cool joy and sleep i' the warm sun,
And men will call me mad, like that old King.

For I am woodland-natured, and have made
Dryads my bedfellows,
And I have played
With the sleek Naiads in the splash of pools
And made a mock of gowned and trousered fools.
Helen, none knows
Better than thou how like a Faun I strayed.
And I am half Faun now, and my heart goes
Out to the forest and the crack of twigs,
The drip of wet leaves and the low soft laughter
Of brooks that chuckle o'er old mossy jests
And say them over to themselves, the nests
Of squirrels and the holes the chipmunk digs,
Where through the branches the slant rays
Dapple with sunlight the leaf-matted ground,
And the wind comes with blown vesture rustling after,
And through the woven lattice of crisp sound
A bird's song lightens like a maiden's face.

O wildwood Helen, let them strive and fret,
Those goggled men with their dissecting-knives!

Let them in charnel-houses pass their lives
And seek in death life's secret! And let
Those hard-faced worldlings prematurely old
Gnaw their thin lips with vain desire to get

Portia's fair fame or Lesbia's carcanet,
Or crown of Caesar or Catullus,
Apicius' lampreys or Crassus' gold!
For these consider many things—but yet
By land nor sea
They shall not find the way to Arcady,
The old home of the awful heart-dear Mother,
Whereto child-dreams and long rememberings lull us,
Far from the cares that overlay and smother
The memories of old woodland out-door mirth
In the dim first life-burst centuries ago,
The sense of the freedom and nearness of Earth—
Nay, this they shall not know;
For who goes thither,
Leaves all the cark and clutch of his soul behind,
The doves defiled and the serpents shrined,
The hates that wax and the hopes that wither;
Nor does he journey, seeking where it be,
But wakes and finds himself in Arcady.

Hist! there's a stir in the brush.
Was it a face through the leaves?
Back of the laurels a skurry and rush
Hillward, then silence except for the thrush
That throws one song from the dark of the bush
And is gone; and I plunge in the wood, and the swift soul
cleaves
Through the swirl and the flow of the leaves,
As a swimmer stands with his white limbs bare to the sun
For the space that a breath is held, and drops in the sea;
And the undulant woodland folds round me, intimate,
fluctuant, free,
Like the clasp and the cling of waters,
and the reach and the effort is done, —
There is only the glory of living, exultant to be.

O goodly damp smell of the ground!
O rough sweet bark of the trees!
O clear sharp cracklings of sound!
O life that's a-thrill and a-bound
With the vigor of boyhood and morning, and the noontide's
rapture of ease!
Was there ever a weary heart in the world?

A lag in the body's urge or a flag of the spirit's wings?
Did a man's heart ever break
For a lost hope's sake?
For here there is lilt in the quiet and calm in the quiver of
things.
Ay, this old oak, gray-grown and knurled,
Solemn and sturdy and big,
Is as young of heart, as alert and elate in his rest,
As the nuthatch there that clings to the tip of the twig
And scolds at the wind that it buffets too rudely its nest.

Oh, what is it breathes in the air?
Oh, what is it touches my cheek?
There's a sense of a presence that lurks in the branches.
But where?
Is it far, is it far to seek?

A ROVER'S SONG.

Snowdrift of the mountains,
Spindrift of the sea,
We who down the border
Rove from gloom to glee, —

Snowdrift of the mountains,
Spindrift of the sea,
There be no such gypsies
Over earth as we.

Snowdrift of the mountains,
Spindrift of the sea,
Let us part the treasure
Of the world in three.

Snowdrift of the mountains,
Spindrift of the sea,
You shall keep your kingdoms;
Joscelyn for me!

DOWN THE SONGO.

I.

Floating!
Floating—and all the stillness waits
And listens at the ivory gates,
Full of a dim uncertain presage
Of some strange, undelivered message.
There is no sound save from the bush
The alto of the shy wood-thrush,
And ever and anon the dip
Of a lazy oar.

The rhythmic drowsiness keeps time
To hazy subtleties of rhyme
That seem to slip
Through the lulled soul to seek the sleepy shore.
The idle clouds go floating by;
Above us sky, beneath us sky;
The sun shines on us as we lie
Floating.

It is a dream.
It is a dream, my love; see how
The ripples quiver at the prow,
And all the long reflections shake
Unsteadily beneath the lake.
The mists about the uplands show
Dim violet towers that come and go.
Phantasmagoric palaces
Rise trembling there,
As though one breath of waking weather
Would crash their airy walls together
With sudden stress,
While silent detonations shook the air—
Vast fabrics toppling to the ground
And vanishing without a sound.
Ah, love, these are not what we deem;
It is a dream.

II.

Let us dream on, then, — —dream and die
Ere the dream pass.
Let us for once, like idle flowers,
Let slip the unregarded hours,
Like the wise flowers that lie
Unfretted by a feeble thought,
Future and past alike forgot,
Drinking the dew contentedly
In the cool grass.

III.

Look yonder where the clouds float; could we glide
As they, across the sky's blue shoreless tide,
What better were it than to dream
Across yon lake and into this still stream?

IV.

Trees and a glimpse of sky!
And the slow river, quiet as a pool!
And thou and I—and thou and I—
Kiss me! How soft the air is and how cool!

THE WANDER-LOVERS.

Down the world with Marna!
That's the life for me!
Wandering with the wandering wind,
Vagabond and unconfined!
Roving with the roving rain
Its unboundaried domain!
Kith and kin of wander-kind,
Children of the sea!

Petrels of the sea-drift!
Swallows of the lea!
Arabs of the whole wide girth
Of the wind-encircled earth!
In all climes we pitch our tents,
Cronies of the elements,
With the secret lords of birth
Intimate and free.

All the seaboard knows us
From Fundy to the Keys;
Every bend and every creek
Of abundant Chesapeake;
Ardise hills and Newport coves
And the far-off orange groves,
Where Floridian oceans break,
Tropic tiger seas.

Down the world with Marna,
Tarrying there and here!
Just as much at home in Spain
As in Tangier or Touraine!
Shakespeare's Avon knows us well,
And the crags of Neufchâtel;
And the ancient Nile is fain
Of our coming near.

Down the world with Marna,
Daughter of the air!
Marna of the subtle grace,

And the vision in her face!
Moving in the measures trod
By the angels before God!
With her sky-blue eyes amaze
And her sea-blue hair!

Marna with the trees' life
In her veins a-stir!
Marna of the aspen heart
Where the sudden quivers start!
Quick-responsive, subtle, wild!
Artless as an artless child,
Spite of all her reach of art!
Oh, to roam with her!

Marna with the wind's will,
Daughter of the sea!
Marna of the quick disdain,
Starting at the dream of stain!
At a smile with love aglow,
At a frown a statued woe,
Standing pinnacled in pain
Till a kiss sets free!

Down the world with Marna,
Daughter of the fire!
Marna of the deathless hope,
Still alert to win new scope
Where the wings of life may spread
For a flight unhazarded!
Dreaming of the speech to cope
With the heart's desire!

Marna of the far quest
After the divine!
Striving ever for some goal
Past the blunder-god's control!
Dreaming of potential years
When no day shall dawn in fears!
That's the Marna of my soul,
Wander-bride of mine!

DISCOVERY.

When the bugler morn shall wind his horn,
And we wake to the wild to be,
Shall we open our eyes on the selfsame skies
And stare at the selfsame sea?
O new, new day! though you bring no stay
To the strain of the sameness grim,
You are new, new, new—new through and through,
And strange as a lawless dream.

Will the driftwood float by the lonely boat
And our prisoner hearts unbar,
As it tells of the strand of an unseen land
That lies not far, not far?
O new, new hope! O sweep and scope
Of the glad, unlying sea!
You are new, new, new—with the promise true
Of the dreamland isles to be.

Will the land-birds fly across the sky,
Though the land is not to see?
Have they dipped and passed in the sea-line vast?
Have we left the land a-lee?
O new despair! I though the hopeless air
Grow foul with the calm and grieves,
You are new, new, new—and we cleave to you
As a soul to its freedom cleaves.

Does the falling night hide fiends to fight
And phantoms to affray?
What demons lurk in the grisly mirk,
As the night-watch waits for day?
O strange new gloom! we await the doom,
And what doom none may deem;
But it's new, new, new—and we'll sail it through,
While the mocking sea-gulls scream.

A light, a light, in the dead of night,
That lifts and sinks in the waves!
What folk are they who have kindled its ray, —

Men or the ghouls of graves?
O new, new fear! near, near and near,
And you bear us weal or woe!
But you're new, new, new — so a cheer for you!
And onward — friend or foe!

Shall the lookout call from the foretop tall,
"Land, land! " with a maddened scream,
And the crew in glee from the taffrail see
Where the island palm-trees dream?
New heart, new eyes! For the morning skies
Are a-chant with their green and gold!
New, new, new, new — new through and through!
New, new till the dawn is old!

A MORE ANCIENT MARINER.

The swarthy bee is a buccaneer,
A burly velveted rover,
Who loves the booming wind in his ear
As he sails the seas of clover.

A waif of the goblin pirate crew,
With not a soul to deplore him,
He steers for the open verge of blue
With the filmy world before him.

His flimsy sails abroad on the wind
Are shivered with fairy thunder;
On a line that sings to the light of his wings
He makes for the lands of wonder.

He harries the ports of the Hollyhocks,
And levies on poor Sweetbrier;
He drinks the whitest wine of Phlox,
And the Rose is his desire.

He hangs in the Willows a night and a day;
He rifles the Buckwheat patches;
Then battens his store of pelf galore
Under the tautest hatches.

He woos the Poppy and weds the Peach,
Inveigles Daffodilly,
And then like a tramp abandons each
For the gorgeous Canada Lily.

There's not a soul in the garden world
But wishes the day were shorter,
When Mariner B. puts out to sea
With the wind in the proper quarter.

Or, so they say! But I have my doubts;
For the flowers are only human,
And the valor and gold of a vagrant bold
Were always dear to woman.

He dares to boast, along the coast,
The beauty of Highland Heather, —
How he and she, with night on the sea,
Lay out on the hills together.

He pilfers from every port of the wind,
From April to golden autumn;
But the thieving ways of his mortal days
Are those his mother taught him.

His morals are mixed, but his will is fixed;
He prospers after his kind,
And follows an instinct, compass-sure,
The philosophers call blind.

And that is why, when he comes to die,
He'll have an easier sentence
Than some one I know who thinks just so,
And then leaves room for repentance.

He never could box the compass round;
He doesn't know port from starboard;
But he knows the gates of the Sundown Straits,
Where the choicest goods are harbored.

He never could see the Rule of Three,
But he knows a rule of thumb
Better than Euclid's, better than yours,
Or the teachers' yet to come.

He knows the smell of the hydromel
As if two and two were five;
And hides it away for a year and a day
In his own hexagonal hive.

Out in the day, hap-hazard, alone,
Booms the old vagrant hummer,
With only his whim to pilot him
Through the splendid vast of summer.

He steers and steers on the slant of the gale,
Like the fiend or Vanderdecken;
And there's never an unknown course to sail

But his crazy log can reckon.

He drones along with his rough sea-song
And the throat of a salty tar,
This devil-may-care, till he makes his lair
By the light of a yellow star.

He looks like a gentleman, lives like a lord,
And works like a Trojan hero;
Then loafs all winter upon his hoard,
With the mercury at zero.

A SONG BY THE SHORE.

"Lose and love" is love's first art;
So it was with thee and me,
For I first beheld thy heart
On the night I last saw thee.
Pine-woods and mysteries!
Sea-sands and sorrows!
Hearts fluttered by a breeze
That bodes dark morrows, morrows, —
Bodes dark morrows!

Moonlight in sweet overflow
Poured upon the earth and sea!
Lovelight with intenser glow
In the deeps of thee and me!
Clasped hands and silences!
Hearts faint and throbbing!
The weak wind sighing in the trees!
The strong surf sobbing, sobbing, —
The strong surf sobbing!

A HILL SONG.

Hills where once my love and I
Let the hours go laughing by!
All your woods and dales are sad, —
You have lost your Oread.
Falling leaves! Silent woodlands!
Half your loveliness is fled.
Golden-rod, wither now!
Winter winds, come hither now!
All the summer joy is dead.

There's a sense of something gone
In the grass I linger on.
There's an under-voice that grieves
In the rustling of the leaves.
Pine-clad peaks! Rushing waters!
Glens where we were once so glad!
There's a light passed from you,
There's a joy outcast from you, —
You have lost your Oread.

AT SEA.

As a brave man faces the foe,
Alone against hundreds, and sees Death grin in his teeth,
But, shutting his lips, fights on to the end
Without speech, without hope, without flinching, —
So, silently, grimly, the steamer
Lurches ahead through the night.

A beacon-light far off,
Twinkling across the waves like a star!
But no star in the dark overhead!
The splash of waters at the prow, and the evil light
Of the death-fires flitting like will-o'-the-wisps beneath! And
beyond
Silence and night!

I sit by the taffrail,
Alone in the dark and the blown cold mist and the spray,
Feeling myself swept on irresistibly,
Sunk in the night and the sea, and made one with their
footfall-less onrush,
Letting myself be borne like a spar adrift
Helplessly into the night.

Without fear, without wish,
Insensate save of a dull, crushed ache in my heart,
Careless whither the steamer is going,
Conscious only as in a dream of the wet and the dark
And of a form that looms and fades indistinctly
Everywhere out of the night.

O love, how came I here?
Shall I wake at thy side and smile at my dream?
The dream that grips me so hard that I cannot wake nor stir!
O love! O my own love, found but to be lost!
My soul sends over the waters a wild inarticulate cry,
Like a gull's scream heard in the night.

The mist creeps closer. The beacon
Vanishes astern. The sea's monotonous noises

Lapse through the drizzle with a listless, subsiding cadence.
And thou, O love, and the sea throb on in my brain together,
While the steamer plunges along,
Butting its way through the night.

ISABEL.

In her body's perfect sweet
Suppleness and languor meet, —
Arms that move like lapsing billows,
Breasts that Love would make his pillows,
Eyes where vision melts in bliss,
Lips that ripen to a kiss.

CONTEMPORARIES.

"A barbered woman's man, " —yes, so
He seemed to me a twelvemonth since;
And so he may be—let it go—
Admit his flaws—we need not wince
To find our noblest not all great.
What of it? He is still the prince,
And we the pages of his state.

The world applauds his words; his fame
Is noised wherever knowledge be;
Even the trader hears his name,
As one far inland hears the sea;
The lady quotes him to the beau
Across a cup of Russian tea;
They know him and they do not know.

I know him. In the nascent years
Men's eyes shall see him as one crowned;
His voice shall gather in their ears
With each new age prophetic sound;
And you and I and all the rest,
Whose brows to-day are laurel-bound,
Shall be but plumes upon his crest.

A year ago this man was poor, —
This Alfred whom the nations praise;
He stood a beggar at my door
For one mere word to help him raise
From fainting limbs and shoulders bent
The burden of the weary days;
And I withheld it—and he went.

I knew him then, as I know now,
Our largest heart, our loftiest mind;
Yet for the curls upon his brow
And for his lisp, I could not find
The helping word, the cheering touch.
Ah, to be just, as well as kind, —
It costs so little and so much!

It seemed unmanly in my sight
That he, whose spirit was so strong
To lead the blind world to the light,
Should look so like the mincing throng
Who advertise the tailor's art.
It angered me—I did him wrong—
I grudged my groat and shut my heart.

I might have been the prophet's friend,
Helped him who is to help the world!
Now, when the striving is at end,
The reek-stained battle-banners furled,
And the age hears its muster-call,
Then I, because his hair was curled,
I shall have lost my chance—that's all.

THE TWO BOBBIES.

Bobbie Burns and Bobbie Browning,
They're the boys I'd like to see.
Though I'm not the boy for Bobbie,
Bobbie is the boy for me!

Bobbie Browning was the good boy;
Turned the language inside out,
Wrote his plays and had his days,
Died—and held his peace, no doubt.

Poor North Bobbie was the bad boy, —
Bad, bad, bad, bad Bobbie Burns!
Loved and made the world his lover,
Kissed and barleycomed by turns.

London's dweller, child of wisdom,
Kept his counsel, took his toll;
Ayrshire's vagrant paid the piper,
Lost the game—God save his soul!

Bobbie Burns and Bobbie Browning,
What's the difference, you see?
Bob the lover, Bob the lawyer;
Bobbie is the boy for me!

A TOAST.

Here's a health to thee, Roberts,
And here's a health to me;
And here's to all the pretty girls
From Denver to the sea!

Here's to mine and here's to thine!
Now's the time to clink it!
Here's a flagon of old wine,
And here are we to drink it.

Wine that maketh glad the heart
Of the bully boy!
Here's the toast that we love most,
"Love and song and joy! "

Song that is the flower of love,
And joy that is the fruit!
Here's the love of woman, lad,
And here's our love to boot!

You and I are far too wise
Not to fill our glasses.
Here's to me and here's to thee,
And here's to all the lasses!

THE KAVANAGH.

A stone jug and a pewter mug,
And a table set for three!
A jug and a mug at every place,
And a biscuit or two with Brie!
Three stone jugs of Cruiskeen Lawn,
And a cheese like crusted foam!
The Kavanagh receives to-night!
McMurrough is at home!

We three and the barley-bree!
And a health to the one away,
Who drifts down careless Italy,
God's wanderer and estray!
For friends are more than Arno's store
Of garnered charm, and he
Were blither with us here the night
Than Titian bids him be.

Throw ope the window to the stars,
And let the warm night in!
Who knows what revelry in Mars
May rhyme with rouse akin?
Fill up and drain the loving cup
And leave no drop to waste!
The moon looks in to see what's up —
Begad, she'd like a taste!

What odds if Leinster's kingly roll
Be now an idle thing?
The world is his who takes his toll,
A vagrant or a king.
What though the crown be melted down,
And the heir a gypsy roam?
The Kavanagh receives to-night!
McMurrough is at home!

We three and the barley-bree!
And the moonlight on the floor!
Who were a man to do with less?

What emperor has more?
Three stone jugs of Cruiskeen Lawn,
And three stout hearts to drain
A slanter to the truth in the heart of youth
And the joy of the love of men.

A CAPTAIN OF THE PRESS-GANG.

Shipmate, leave the ghostly shadows,
Where thy boon companions throng!
We will put to sea together
Through the twilight with a song.

Leering closer, rank and girding,
In this Black Port where we bide,
Reel a thousand flaring faces;
But escape is on the tide.

Let the tap-rooms of the city
Reek till the red dawn comes round.
There is better wine in plenty
On the cruise where we are bound.

I've aboard a hundred messmates
Better than these 'long-shore knaves.
There is wreckage on the shallows;
It's the open sea that saves.

Hark, lad, dost not hear it calling?
That's the voice thy father knew,
When he took the King's good cutlass
In his grip, and fought it through.

Who would palter at press-money
When he heard that sea-cry vast?
That's the call makes lords of lubbers,
When they ship before the mast.

Let thy cronies of the tavern
Keep their kisses bought with gold;
On the high seas there are regions
Where the heart is never old,

Where the great winds every morning
Sweep the sea-floor clean and white,
And upon the steel-blue arches
Burnish the great stars of night;

There the open hand will lose not,
  Nor the loosened tongue betray.
  Signed, and with our sailing orders,
  We will clear before the day;

On the shining yards of heaven
  See a wider dawn unfurled....
  The eternal slaves of beauty
  Are the masters of the world.

THE BUCCANEERS.

Oh, not for us the easy mirth
Of men that never roam!
The crackling of the narrow hearth,
The cabined joys of home!
Keep your tame, regulated glee,
O pale protected State!
Our dwelling-place is on the sea,
Our joy the joy of Fate!

No long caresses give us ease,
No lazy languors warm,
We seize our mates as the sea-gulls seize,
And leave them to the storm.
But in the bridal halls of gloom
The couch is stern and strait;
For us the marriage rite of Doom,
The nuptial joy of Fate.

Wine for the weaklings of the town,
Their lucky toasts to drain!
Our skoal for them whose star goes down,
Our drink the drink of men!
No Bacchic ivy for our brows!
Like vikings, we await
The grim, ungarlanded carouse
We keep to-night with Fate.

Ho, gamesters of the pampered court!
What stakes are those at strife?
Your thousands are but paltry sport
To them that play for life.
You risk doubloons, and hold your breath.
Win groats, and wax elate;
But we throw loaded dice with Death,
And call the turn on Fate.

The kings of earth are crowned with care,
Their poets wail and sigh;
Our music is to do and dare,

Our empire is to die.
Against the storm we fling our glee
And shout, till Time abate
The exultation of the sea,
The fearful joy of Fate.

THE WAR-SONG OF GAMELBAR.

Bowmen, shout for Gamelbar!
Winds, unthrottle the wolves of war!
Heave a breath
And dare a death
For the doom of Gamelbar!
Wealth for Gamel,
Wine for Gamel,
Crimson wine for Gamelbar!

CHORUS: —Oh, sleep for a knave,
          With his sins in the sod!
          And death for the brave,
          With his glory up to God!
          And joy for the girl,
          And ease for the churl!
          But the great game of war
          For our lord Gamelbar,
          Gamelbar!

Spearmen, shout for Gamelbar,
With his Saxon thirty score!
Heave a sword
For our overlord,
Lord of warriors, Gamelbar!
Life for Gamel,
Love for Gamel,
Lady-loves for Gamelbar!

Horsemen, shout for Gamelbar!
Swim the ford and climb the scaur!
Heave a hand
For the maiden land,
The maiden land of Gamelbar!
Glory for Gamel,
Gold for Gamel,
Yellow gold for Gamelbar!

Armorers for Gamelbar,
Rivet and forge and fear no scar!

Heave a hammer
With anvil clamor,
To weld and brace for Gamelbar!
Ring for Gamel!
Rung for Gamel!
Ring-rung-ring for Gamelbar!

Yeomen, shout for Gamelbar,
And his battle-hand in war!
Heave his pennon;
Cheer his men on,
In the ranks of Gamelbar!
Strength for Gamel,
Song for Gamel,
One war-song for Gamelbar!

Roncliffe, shout for Gamelbar!
Menthorpe, Bryan, Castelfar!
Heave, Thorparch
Of the Waving Larch,
And Spofford's thane, for Gamelbar!
Blaise for Gamel,
Brame for Gamel,
Rougharlington for Gamelbar!

Maidens; strew for Gamelbar
Roses down his way to war!
Heave a handful,
Fill the land full
Of your gifts to Gamelbar!
Dream of Gamel,
Dance for Gamel,
Dance in the halls for Gamelbar!

Servitors, shout for Gamelbar!
Roast the ox and stick the boar!
Heave a bone
To gaunt Harone,
The great war-hound of Gamelbar!
Mead for Gamel,
Mirth for Gamel,
Mirth at the board for Gamelbar!

Trumpets, speak for Gamelbar!
Blare as ye never blared before!
Heave a bray
In the horns to-day,
The red war-horns of Gamelbar!
To-night for Gamel,
The North for Gamel,
With fires on the hills for Gamelbar!

Shout for Gamel, Gamelbar,
Till your throats can shout no more!
Heave a cry
As he rideth by,
Sons of Orm, for Gamelbar!
Folk for Gamel,
Fame for Gamel,
Years and fame for Gamelbar!

CHORUS: —Oh, sleep for a knave
            With his sins in the sod!
            And death for the brave,
            With his glory up to God!
            And joy for the girl,
            And ease for the churl!
            But the great game of war
            For our lord Gamelbar,
            Gamelbar!

THE OUTLAW.

Oh, let my lord laugh in his halls
When he the tale shall tell!
But woe to Jarlwell and its walls
When I shall laugh as well!
And he that laughs the last, lads,
Laughs well, laughs well!

He's lord of many a burg and farm
And mickle thralls and gold,
And I am but my own right arm,
My dwelling-place the wold.
But when we twain meet face to face,
He will hot laugh so bold.

The shame he chuckles as he shows
This time he need not tell;
I'll give his body to the crows,
And his black soul to Hell.
For he that laughs the last, lads,
Laughs well, laughs well!

THE KING'S SON.

"Daughter, daughter, marry no man,
Though a king's son come to woo,
If he be not more than blessing or ban
To the secret soul of you. "

"'Tis the King's son, indeed, I ween,
And he left me even but now,
And he shall make me a dazzling queen,
With a gold crown on my brow. "

"And are you one that a golden crown,
Or the lust of a name can lure?
You had better wed with a country clown,
And keep your young heart pure. "

"Mother, the King has sworn, and said
That his son shall wed but me;
And I must gang to the prince's bed,
Or a traitor I shall be. "

"Oh, what care you for an old man's wrath?
Or what care you for a king?
I had rather you fled on an outlaw's path,
A rebel, a hunted thing. "

"Mother, it is my father's will,
For the King has promised him fair
A goodly earldom of hollow and hill,
And a coronet to wear. "

"Then woe is worth a father's name,
For it names your dourest foe!
I had rather you came the child of shame
Than to have you fathered so. "

"Mother, I shall have gold enow,
Though love be never mine,
To buy all else that the world can show
Of good and fair and fine. "

"Oh, what care you for a prince's gold,
Or the key of a kingdom's till?
I had rather see you a harlot bold
That sins of her own free will.

"For I have been wife for the stomach's sake,
And I know whereof I say;
A harlot is sold for a passing slake,
But a wife is sold for aye.

"Body and soul for a lifetime sell,
And the price of the sale shall be
That you shall be harlot and slave as well
Until Death set you free. "

LAURANA'S SONG. FOR "A LADY OF VENICE. "

Who'll have the crumpled pieces of a heart?
Let him take mine!
Who'll give his whole of passion for a part,
And call't divine?
Who'll have the soiled remainder of desire?
Who'll warm his fingers at a burnt-out fire?
Who'll drink the lees of love, and cast i' the mire
The nobler wine?

Let him come here, and kiss me on the mouth,
And have his will!
Love dead and dry as summer in the South
When winds are still
And all the leafage shrivels in the heat!
Let him come here and linger at my feet
Till he grow weary with the over-sweet,
And die, or kill.

LAUNA DEE.

Weary, oh, so weary
With it all!
Sunny days or dreary—
How they pall!
Why should we be heroes,
Launa Dee,
Striving to no winning?
Let the world be Zero's!
As in the beginning
Let it be!

What good comes of toiling,
When all's done?
Frail green sprays for spoiling
Of the sun;
Laurel leaf or myrtle,
Love or fame—
Ah, what odds what spray, sweet?
Time, that makes life fertile,
Makes its blooms decay, sweet,
As they came.

Lie here with me dreaming,
Cheek to cheek,
Lithe limbs twined and gleaming,
Brown and sleek;
Like two serpents coiling
In their lair.
Where's the good of wreathing
Sprays for Time's despoiling?
Let me feel your breathing
In my hair.

You and I together—
Was it so?
In the August weather
Long ago!
Did we kiss and fellow,
Side by side,

Till the sunbeams quickened
From our stalks great yellow
Sunflowers, till we sickened
There and died?

Were we tigers creeping
Through the glade
Where our prey lay sleeping,
Unafraid,
In some Eastern jungle?
Better so.
I am sure the snarling
Beasts could never bungle
Life as men do, darling,
Who half know.

Ah, if all of life, love,
Were the living!
Just to cease from strife, love,
And from grieving;
Let the swift world pass us,
You and me,
Stilled from all aspiring, —
Sinai nor Parnassus
Longer worth desiring,
Launa Dee!

Just to live like lilies
In the lake!
Where no thought nor will is,
To mistake!
Just to lose the human
Eyes that weep!
Just to cease from seeming
Longer man and woman!
Just to reach the dreaming
And the sleep!

THE MENDICANTS.

We are as mendicants who wait
Along the roadside in the sun.
Tatters of yesterday and shreds
Of morrow clothe us every one.

And some are dotards, who believe
And glory in the days of old;
While some are dreamers, harping still
Upon an unknown age of gold.

Hopeless or witless! Not one heeds,
As lavish Time comes down the way
And tosses in the suppliant hat
One great new-minted gold To-day.

Ungrateful heart and grudging thanks,
His beggar's wisdom only sees
Housing and bread and beer enough;
He knows no other things than these.

O foolish ones, put by your care!
Where wants are many, joys are few;
And at the wilding springs of peace,
God keeps an open house for you.

But that some Fortunatus' gift
Is lying there within his hand,
More costly than a pot of pearls,
His dulness does not understand.

And so his creature heart is filled;
His shrunken self goes starved away.
Let him wear brand-new garments still,
Who has a threadbare soul, I say.

But there be others, happier few,
The vagabondish sons of God,
Who know the by-ways and the flowers,
And care not how the world may plod.

They idle down the traffic lands,
And loiter through the woods with spring;
To them the glory of the earth
Is but to hear a bluebird sing.

They too receive each one his Day;
But their wise heart knows many things
Beyond the sating of desire,
Above the dignity of kings.

One I remember kept his coin,
And laughing flipped it in the air;
But when two strolling pipe-players
Came by, he tossed it to the pair.

Spendthrift of joy, his childish heart
Danced to their wild outlandish bars;
Then supperless he laid him down
That night, and slept beneath the stars.

THE MARCHING MORROWS.

Now gird thee well for courage,
My knight of twenty year,
Against the marching morrows
That fill the world with fear!

The flowers fade before them;
The summer leaves the hill;
Their trumpets range the morning,
And those who hear grow still.

Like pillagers of harvest,
Their fame is far abroad,
As gray remorseless troopers
That plunder and maraud.

The dust is on their corselets;
Their marching fills the world;
With conquest after conquest
Their banners are unfurled.

They overthrow the battles
Of every lord of war,
From world-dominioned cities
Wipe out the names they bore.

Sohrab, Rameses, Roland,
Ramoth, Napoleon, Tyre,
And the Romeward Huns of Attila—
Alas, for their desire!

By April and by autumn
They perish in their pride,
And still they close and gather
Out of the mountain-side.

The tanned and tameless children
Of the wild elder earth,
With stature of the northlights,
They have the stars for girth.

There's not a hand to stay them,
Of all the hearts that brave;
No captain to undo them,
No cunning to off-stave.

Yet fear thou not! If haply
Thou be the kingly one,
They'll set thee in their vanguard
To lead them round the sun.

IN THE WORKSHOP.

Once in the Workshop, ages ago,
The clay was wet and the fire was low.

And He who was bent on fashioning man
Moulded a shape from a clod,
And put the loyal heart therein;
While another stood watching by.

"What's that? " said Beelzebub.
"A lover, " said God.
And Beelzebub frowned, for he knew that kind.

And then God fashioned a fellow shape
As lithe as a willow rod,
And gave it the merry roving eye
And the range of the open road.

"What's that? " said Beelzebub.
"A vagrant, " said God.
And Beelzebub smiled, for he knew that kind.

And last of all God fashioned a form,
And gave it, what was odd,
The loyal heart and the roving eye;
And he whistled, light of care.

"What's that? " said Beelzebub.
"A poet, " said God.
And Beelzebub frowned, for he did not know.

THE MOTE.

Two shapes of august bearing, seraph tall,
Of indolent imperturbable regard,
Stood in the Tavern door to drink. As the first
Lifted his glass to let the warm light melt
In the slow bubbles of the wine, a sunbeam,
Red and broad as smouldering autumn, smote
Down through its mystery; and a single fleck,
The tiniest sun-mote settling through the air,
Fell on the grape-dark surface and there swam.

Gently the Drinker with fastidious care
Stretched hand to clear the speck away. "No, no! " —
His comrade stayed his arm. "Why, " said the first,
"What would you have me do? " "Ah, let it float
A moment longer! " And the second smiled.
"Do you not know what that is? " "No, indeed. "
"A mere dust-mote, a speck of soot, you think,
A plague-germ still unsatisfied. It is not.
That is the Earth. See, I will stretch my hand
Between it and the sun; the passing shadow
Gives its poor dwellers a glacial period.
Let it but stand an hour, it would dissolve,
Intangible as the color of the wine.
There, throw it away now! Lift it from the sweet
Enveloping flood it has enjoyed so well; "
(He smiled as only those who live can smile)
"Its time is done, its revelry complete,
Its being accomplished. Let us drink again. "

56

IN THE HOUSE OF IDIEDAILY.

Oh, but life went gayly, gayly,
In the house of Idiedaily!

There were always throats to sing
Down the river-banks with spring,

When the stir of heart's desire
Set the sapling's heart on fire.

Bobolincolns in the meadows,
Leisure in the purple shadows,

Till the poppies without number
Bowed their heads in crimson slumber,

And the twilight came to cover
Every unreluctant lover.

Not a night but some brown maiden
Bettered all the dusk she strayed in,

While the roses in her hair
Bankrupted oblivion there.

Oh, but life went gayly, gayly,
In the house of Idiedaily!

But this hostelry, The Barrow,
With its chambers, bare and narrow,

Mean, ill-windowed, damp, and wormy,
Where the silence makes you squirmy,

And the guests are never seen to,
Is a vile place, a mere lean-to,

Not a traveller speaks well of,
Even worse than I heard tell of,

Mouldy, ramshackle, and foul.
What a dwelling for a soul!

Oh, but life went gayly, gayly,
In the house of Idiedaily!

There the hearth was always warm,
From the slander of the storm.

There your comrade was your neighbor,
Living on to-morrow's labor.

And the board was always steaming,
Though Sir Ringlets might be dreaming.

Not a plate but scoffed at porridge,
Not a cup but floated borage.

There were always jugs of sherry
Waiting for the makers merry,

And the dark Burgundian wine
That would make a fool divine.

Oh, but life went gayly, gayly
In the house of Idiedaily!

RESIGNATION.

When I am only fit to go to bed,
Or hobble out to sit within the sun,
Ring down the curtain, say the play is done,
And the last petals of the poppy shed!

I do not want to live when I am old,
I have no use for things I cannot love;
And when the day that I am talking of
(Which God forfend!) is come, it will be cold.

But if there is another place than this,
Where all the men will greet me as "Old Man, "
And all the women wrap me in a smile,
Where money is more useless than a kiss,
And good wine is not put beneath the ban,
I will go there and stay a little while.

COMRADES.

Comrades, pour the wine to-night
For the parting is with dawn!
Oh, the clink of cups together,
With the daylight coming on!
Greet the morn
With a double horn,
When strong men drink together!

Comrades, gird your swords to-night,
For the battle is with dawn!
Oh, the clash of shields together,
With the triumph coming on!
Greet the foe,
And lay him low,
When strong men fight together!

Comrades, watch the tides to-night,
For the sailing is with dawn!
Oh, to face the spray together,
With the tempest coming on!
Greet the sea
With a shout of glee,
When strong men roam together!

Comrades, give a cheer to-night,
For the dying is with dawn!
Oh, to meet the stars together,
With the silence coming on!
Greet the end
As a friend a friend,
When strong men die together!

THE END.

Made in the USA
Las Vegas, NV
07 November 2022